The Goshen Factor

From Slavery to Soldier-Servant of the Most High God

By Joyce Toney

ISBN:979-8-9940160-7-7

THE GOSHEN FACTOR

From Slavery to Soldier-Servant of the Most High God

Protection. Provision. Distinction. Authority.

"So that you may know that the Lord makes a distinction between Egypt and Israel" (Exodus 11:7 AMP).

Why Goshen Matters

Goshen matters because it reveals how God governs outcomes in the midst of crisis. In Egypt, the same plagues fell on the same land at the same time, yet the results were not the same for everyone. Egypt experienced loss, darkness, fear, and death. Goshen remained protected, provided for, and preserved. This difference was not accidental. It was intentional and governed by God's authority (Exodus 8:22 AMP).

Goshen was not favoritism, and it did not escape. It was a covenant position. God declared that He would place a distinction between His people and Egypt so that His power, **ownership**, and authority would be known. ***Where God established distinction***, judgment could not cross (Exodus 9:4 AMP).

The Goshen Factor explains why two people can experience the same world, the same pressure, and the same crisis, yet live under completely different outcomes. The environment did not determine the result. **Alignment** did.

Scripture records that this distinction was so complete that even hostility was restrained. God declared that not even a dog would lift up its voice against the Israelites, so that all would know that the Lord makes a distinction between Egypt and Israel (Exodus 11:7 AMP). No accusation, no alarm, and no threat was permitted to rise against God's people. Creation itself obeyed God's boundary.

Goshen also reveals that God was preparing His people, not just protecting them. While Israel lived under covering, God was preserving their identity so they could move from slavery into purpose. Goshen became the place where redemption was protected until deliverance was complete (Exodus 13:3 AMP).

Goshen is not a geographic location. **It is a spiritual position**. Wherever God's covenant is honored, His authority establishes boundaries, restrains destruction, and provides what is needed. This governing principle is the **Goshen Factor**.

Distinction

When God Draws the Line and Judgment Stops

Distinction is God's deliberate act of separation that establishes **ownership**, protection, and authority. God did not remove Israel from Egypt before judgment began. He drew a line within the land and declared that judgment would not cross it. Where God established distinction, destruction was restrained (Exodus 8:22 AMP).

This distinction was not based on human strength or merit. It was **covenant alignment**. God declared that He would make a distinction between His people and Egypt so that His authority would be clearly revealed. The difference was not location. **The difference was who belonged to God** (Exodus 9:4 AMP).

Darkness covered Egypt, yet the Israelites had light in their dwellings. Judgment moved freely through Egypt, but it stopped at the boundary God established. Distinction functioned as a spiritual boundary enforced by divine authority (Exodus 10:23 AMP).

God's distinction was so complete that even hostility was restrained. Not even a dog was permitted to lift its voice against Israel. No warning cry, no threat, and no agitation were allowed. God silenced every opposing voice so that His people would rest in peace while judgment passed elsewhere (Exodus 11:7 AMP).

Distinction declares ownership. What God claims, He guards. What He guards, judgment cannot trespass. Goshen teaches that protection is governed, not random. When God draws the line, darkness honors it and destruction obeys it.

Slavery

Life Under a Master That Consumes Without Restoring

Before deliverance, Israel lived under slavery in Egypt. Slavery stripped them of rest, identity, voice, and inheritance. Pharaoh's system consumed their strength without restoring purpose. They labored continually and received nothing in return but exhaustion and fear (Exodus 1:13–14 AMP).

Slavery in Scripture represents life under a dominating authority that governs without covenant care. It is submission to a master that takes but does not give, demands but does not protect, and rules without mercy. Egypt was such a system. Living in a system that is not under the government of the Kingdom of God is the same Egyptian system.

God heard the cries of His people and remembered His covenant. Deliverance was not merely rescue from hardship. It was a transfer of authority. God was preparing to remove Israel from under Pharaoh's rule and place them under His own governance (Exodus 6:5–6 AMP).

Slavery had to be broken before purpose could be revealed. Identity had to be restored before assignment could begin. Goshen preserved Israel so that redemption could move them forward.

The Ten Plagues and God's Deliverance Through Distinction and Obedience

Water Turned to Blood: God struck the Nile, Egypt's source of life, revealing that false systems cannot give life. Fish died, and the river became a source of death. God preserved Israel by establishing distinction. The waters in Goshen were not corrupted because God had drawn a boundary around His people, and judgment could not cross it (Exodus 7:20–21; Exodus 8:22 AMP).

Frogs: Frogs overran Egypt, entering homes, beds, and daily life, turning what was considered sacred into a burden. God delivered Israel by restraining the plague from entering Goshen. Obedience and covenant alignment kept disruption outside God's boundary (Exodus 8:1–6; Exodus 8:22 AMP).

Gnats or Lice: Insects rose from the dust and afflicted people and animals, demonstrating God's authority over creation itself. Israel was spared because God had set them apart. Distinction prevented affliction from touching those under covenant protection (Exodus 8:16–19; Exodus 8:22 AMP).

Swarms of Flies: Flies corrupted the land and brought decay, confusion, and unrest throughout Egypt. God declared that Goshen would be exempt so that His authority would be clearly known. The plague stopped at the boundary God established (Exodus 8:20–24; Exodus 8:22 AMP).

Pestilence on Livestock: Egypt's livestock were struck, destroying economic strength and security. God protected Israel's animals completely. Not one belonging to Israel died, proving that provision is preserved where covenant alignment exists (Exodus 9:1–7; Exodus 9:4 AMP).

Boils: Painful boils afflicted people and animals, revealing the collapse of Egypt's false gods of healing. Israel was not afflicted because God restrained the plague within His boundary. God's protection extended to health and wellbeing (Exodus 9:8–12 AMP).

Hail and Fire: Hail mixed with fire devastated crops, livestock, and people throughout Egypt. Goshen remained untouched. God shielded His people from environmental judgment because they were aligned with His covenant (Exodus 9:22–26 AMP).

Locusts: Locusts consumed what remained after the hail, stripping Egypt of sustenance and hope. God preserved Israel's provision. What judgment consumed elsewhere was restrained where

God had drawn the line (Exodus 10:12–15; Exodus 10:23 AMP).

Darkness: Thick darkness covered Egypt, a darkness so heavy it could be felt. Yet Israel had light in their dwellings. God delivered His people by providing clarity, peace, and presence where He ruled (Exodus 10:21–23 AMP).

Death of the Firstborn: Judgment passed through Egypt, bringing death to the firstborn. God instructed Israel to apply blood to the doorposts in obedience. Where the blood was applied, God did not allow the destroyer to enter. Obedience activated protection and covenant restrained judgment (Exodus 12:12–13; Exodus 12:23 AMP).

The Goshen Truth

The plagues reveal that God does not judge blindly.
He governs with authority.
Distinction restrained judgment.
Obedience activated protection.
Covenant preserved life.

God delivered His people not by removing the crisis, but by **governing the outcome**.

This is the Goshen Factor.

The Ten Plagues and God's Protection in Goshen

Plague in Egypt	God's Protection in Goshen
Water turned to blood. The Nile was struck, fish died, and Egypt's source of life became death (Exodus 7:20–21 AMP).	Goshen's water remained untouched. God preserved life where He had established distinction (Exodus 8:22 AMP).
Frogs covered the land, invading homes, beds, and daily life (Exodus 8:1–6 AMP).	Frogs did not invade Goshen. God restrained disruption within covenant boundaries (Exodus 8:22 AMP).

Plague in Egypt	God's Protection in Goshen
Gnats or lice rose from the dust, afflicting people and animals (Exodus 8:16–19 AMP).	Goshen was spared. God demonstrated authority over creation and territory (Exodus 8:22 AMP).
Swarms of flies corrupted the land, bringing decay and chaos (Exodus 8:20–24 AMP).	God set Goshen apart so that no swarms entered Israel's dwellings (Exodus 8:22 AMP).
Pestilence killed Egyptian livestock, destroying economic strength	Not one animal belonging to Israel died. God protected provision and livelihood (Exodus 9:4 AMP).

Plague in Egypt	God's Protection in Goshen
(Exodus 9:1–7 AMP).	
Painful boils afflicted people and animals, revealing the collapse of Egypt's healing gods (Exodus 9:8–12 AMP).	Israel remained unaffected, demonstrating God's restraint of affliction (Exodus 9:11 AMP).
Hail mixed with fire devastated the land, destroying crops and lives (Exodus 9:22–26 AMP).	Goshen was untouched. God shielded His people from environmental judgment (Exodus 9:26 AMP).
Locusts consumed what	Goshen was preserved. God

Plague in Egypt	God's Protection in Goshen
remained, leaving Egypt stripped and desolate (Exodus 10:12–15 AMP).	maintained provision within covenant boundaries (Exodus 10:23 AMP).
Thick darkness covered Egypt, a darkness that could be felt (Exodus 10:21–23 AMP).	Israel had light in their dwellings. God provided clarity and peace where He ruled (Exodus 10:23 AMP).
Death of the firstborn passed through Egypt (Exodus 12:29–30 AMP).	The blood on the doorposts restrained the destroyer. God did not allow entry where covenant was marked (Exodus 12:13; Exodus 12:23 AMP).

The Goshen Truth

The same land experienced judgment and protection at the same time.
The difference was not location.
The difference was **covenant alignment and divine distinction**.

The plagues reveal that God does not judge blindly.
He governs with authority.
Distinction restrained judgment.
Obedience activated protection.
Covenant preserved life.

God delivered His people not by removing the crisis, but by **governing the outcome**.
This is the Goshen Factor.

The Blood on the Doorpost

The Covenant Marker That Restrains the Destroyer

The turning point in Egypt came when God commanded Israel to place blood on the doorposts of their homes. The blood was not symbolic emotion. It was a covenant marker. God declared that when He saw the blood, judgment would pass over the house (Exodus 12:13 AMP).

Scripture states that God Himself would not allow the destroyer to enter a house marked by the blood. Destruction was restrained by divine command. The blood testified before heaven and enforced a boundary judgment could not cross (Exodus 12:23 AMP).

The blood did not plead. It declared covenant ownership. Where the blood was applied in obedience, protection was enforced. This revealed that redemption is not accidental. It is authorized.

From Slaves to Soldier-Servants

Redeemed to Serve the Lord of Hosts

Israel did not leave Egypt as fugitives. They left as a redeemed people. God declared that He delivered them from bondage so they would serve Him. This was not loss of freedom. It was restoration of purpose (Exodus 19:4–6 AMP).

God revealed Himself as a warrior, the Lord of Hosts. Under Jehovah Sabaoth, Israel was no longer a slave people. They were a people under divine command and protection. They moved from forced service under Pharaoh to willing service under God (Exodus 15:3 AMP).

A soldier-servant serves under authority, carries assignment, and is protected by the One who commands. Redemption transformed Israel’s identity and positioned them for purpose.

The Hedge and the Wall of Fire

Boundaries and the Presence of God

God establishes boundaries around what belongs to Him. Scripture describes a hedge that restricts unauthorized access and preserves covenant alignment. Where the hedge stands, destruction is restrained (Hosea 2:6 AMP).

God also declares Himself to be a wall of fire around His people and the glory in their midst. This is not passive protection. It is God's active presence standing guard over what belongs to Him (Zechariah 2:5 AMP).

The Goshen Factor reaches fullness here. God does not merely assign protection. He becomes the protection.

Goshen Today

A Covenant Position

Goshen is not limited to history. It is a covenant position available today. Through Jesus Christ, the Lamb of God, redemption, protection, and purpose are extended to all who believe. Christ is our Passover, and His blood establishes covenant covering (1 Corinthians 5:7 AMP).

Those who belong to God are no longer slaves to sin. They are redeemed, guarded, and commissioned to live under divine authority.

The First Step: Entering Covenant Through New Birth and Union With Christ

1. The New Birth by the Spirit of God

The Goshen Factor begins with spiritual rebirth. A person must be born again by the Spirit of God to enter covenant alignment. This new birth is not reform or religious effort. It is transformation initiated by God, where the spirit is made alive to Him and transferred into His Kingdom (John 3:3–6 AMP; Titus 3:5 AMP).

Without new birth, there is no covenant position.
Goshen begins with spiritual life.

2. Baptism in Water

Water baptism is the outward act of obedience that follows new birth. It represents identification with Christ's death, burial, and separation from the old life of slavery to sin. Baptism does not save by itself, but it marks obedience, surrender, and public identification with Christ (Romans 6:3–4 AMP; Acts 2:38 AMP).

Water baptism declares that the old life no longer rules.
A new life has begun.

3. Baptism in the Holy Spirit

The baptism in the Holy Spirit empowers the believer to live the new life God has given. Jesus promised that the Holy Spirit would clothe believers with power from on high. This baptism equips the believer with spiritual authority, boldness, and the ability to walk in obedience and discernment (Acts 1:4–8 AMP; Luke 24:49 AMP).

The Holy Spirit is God's indwelling presence.
Power accompanies covenant.

4. Baptism Into Christ's Death, Resurrection, and Ascension

Through faith, the believer is united with Christ not only in His death, but also in His resurrection and ascension. Scripture declares that believers have been raised with Christ and seated with Him in heavenly places. This position establishes authority, identity, and victory over spiritual opposition (Romans 6:5 AMP; Ephesians 2:6 AMP; Colossians 3:1–3 AMP).

This is the governing position of Goshen today.
Believers are not beneath the storm.
They are seated with Christ above it.

Why This Step Is Essential to the Goshen Factor

The Goshen Factor does not operate through self-effort.
It operates through **union with Christ**.

New birth establishes life.
Water baptism establishes obedience.
Baptism in the Holy Spirit establishes power.
Union with Christ establishes authority.

Only after this foundation is established can the Goshen Factor be implemented consistently in daily life.

The Second Step: Living Under Covenant Authority

After entering covenant through new birth and union with Christ, the Goshen Factor is activated and sustained through **covenant authority**. God does not merely give life. He grants authority to live protected, governed, and victorious. This authority is exercised through the **blood of Jesus**, the **name of Jesus**, the **Word of God**, and the **Holy Spirit**.

1. The Authority of the Blood of Jesus

The blood of Jesus establishes covenant ownership and legal protection. Scripture declares that believers overcome by the blood of the Lamb. The blood does not beg for mercy. It testifies before God, restrains judgment, and silences accusation. Where the blood speaks, the enemy has no legal claim (Revelation 12:11 AMP; Hebrews 12:24 AMP).

The blood establishes peace with God and secures access to His presence. It is the foundation of protection and deliverance (Colossians 1:20 AMP; Hebrews 9:12 AMP).

2. The Authority of the Name of Jesus

God has exalted the name of Jesus above every name and placed all authority in heaven and on earth under His rule. Believers are authorized to use the name of Jesus to stand against darkness, resist the enemy, and walk in victory. The name represents Christ's authority, not human strength (Philippians 2:9–11 AMP; Luke 10:19 AMP).

When the name of Jesus is spoken in faith, heaven recognizes it and darkness must respond (Acts 3:6 AMP; Mark 16:17 AMP).

3. The Authority of the Word of God

The Word of God is the governing truth that establishes boundaries and exposes deception. Scripture declares that God watches over His Word to perform it. The Word is living, active, and authoritative. Where the Word is believed, spoken, and obeyed, spiritual authority is enforced (Hebrews 4:12 AMP; Jeremiah 1:12 AMP).

The Word defines identity, corrects alignment, and resists the enemy. Jesus Himself overcame temptation by declaring the Word of God (Matthew 4:4 AMP).

4. The Authority of the Holy Spirit

The Holy Spirit is the active presence of God within the believer. He empowers obedience, provides discernment, and enforces Kingdom authority. Scripture declares that where the Spirit of the Lord is, there is freedom. The Spirit leads believers into truth and equips them to walk in power (2 Corinthians 3:17 AMP; John 16:13 AMP).

The Holy Spirit does not replace the Word or the name of Jesus. He enforces them. Power flows through alignment with His leading (Romans 8:14 AMP; Acts 1:8 AMP).

Why This Step Sustains the Goshen Factor

The Goshen Factor is not maintained by fear or isolation.
It is sustained through **covenant authority exercised daily**.

The blood establishes protection.
The name enforces authority.
The Word governs truth.
The Spirit empowers obedience.

Where these operate together, judgment is restrained, peace is established, and purpose is protected.

The Third Step: Maintaining Distinction Through Obedience, Holiness, and Trust

The Goshen Factor is not sustained by momentary faith. It is maintained through a daily life of obedience, holiness, and trust in God's authority. Distinction remains in place when covenant alignment is honored. When obedience is practiced, boundaries remain intact and protection is preserved.

1. Obedience Preserves Distinction

God's protection over Israel was maintained because they obeyed His instructions. Obedience was not partial or delayed. It was immediate and exact. Where obedience was present, judgment was restrained and peace remained.

Obedience demonstrates trust in God's authority rather than reliance on personal understanding (Exodus 12:28 AMP; Deuteronomy 28:1–2 AMP).

Obedience keeps the boundary secure. Disobedience weakens alignment.

2. Holiness Sustains God's Covering

Holiness is not separation from people. It is separation unto God. Scripture declares that God calls His people to be holy because He is holy. Holiness preserves spiritual sensitivity and keeps the believer aligned with God's presence. Where holiness is pursued, God's covering remains active (Leviticus 20:26 AMP; 1 Peter 1:15–16 AMP).

Holiness protects the heart from compromise and guards the covenant position established by God.

3. Trust Replaces Fear

Fear is the enemy of Goshen. God silenced every threatening voice against Israel so that they could rest while judgment passed elsewhere. Trust anchors the believer in God's sovereignty and removes anxiety about outcomes. Those who trust in the Lord dwell securely and are not shaken by surrounding turmoil (Exodus 14:13–14 AMP; Proverbs 3:5–6 AMP).

Trust allows God to govern outcomes without interference.

4. Separation From Worldly Systems

Israel was preserved in Goshen while Egypt's systems collapsed. God calls His people to live differently, not in isolation, but in alignment. Distinction requires refusing to adopt values, behaviors, and dependencies that conflict with God's truth

(Romans 12:2 AMP; 2 Corinthians 6:17 AMP).

Living distinctly maintains spiritual authority and clarity.

5. Continual Dependence on God

The Goshen Factor is sustained through humility and dependence on God. Pride and self-reliance weaken spiritual covering. Scripture declares that God gives grace to the humble and resists the proud. Dependence keeps the believer under God's governance and protection (James 4:6 AMP; Psalm 127:1 AMP).

Dependence invites God's continued involvement.

Why This Step Matters

Distinction is not a moment.
It is a maintained position.

Obedience keeps the boundary intact.
Holiness preserves alignment.
Trust secures peace.

Where these are practiced, the Goshen Factor remains active

and effective in daily life.

The Fourth Step: Walking in Provision, Peace, Holiness, and Mature Purpose Under God's Authority

The Goshen Factor does not end with protection. God preserves His people so they may be **formed into His image and likeness**, walking in holiness, maturity, peace, and divine purpose. Protection creates space for transformation. God guards what He intends to perfect.

1. Provision That Sustains Transformation

God sustained Israel in Goshen so they would not be consumed by fear, lack, or distraction while He prepared them for purpose. Provision is not merely survival. It supports spiritual growth and maturity.

Scripture declares that God supplies what is needed so His people can walk fully in His will (Exodus 16:4 AMP; Philippians 4:19 AMP).

Provision removes anxiety so transformation can continue.

2. Peace That Guards the Heart and Mind

God established peace in Goshen while judgment unfolded elsewhere. Peace is not the absence of conflict. It is the presence of God's governance. Scripture declares that God's peace guards the heart and mind, keeping the believer steady and responsive to His will (Exodus 11:7 AMP; Philippians 4:6–7 AMP).

Peace protects spiritual focus and stability.

3. Holiness That Preserves Alignment

Holiness is separation unto God. God calls His people to be holy because He is holy. Holiness maintains sensitivity to God's voice and preserves alignment with His presence. Where holiness is pursued, God's covering remains active and His purpose is protected (Leviticus 20:26 AMP; 1 Peter 1:15–16 AMP).

Holiness keeps the covenant position intact.

4. Perfection as Maturity in Christ

Biblical perfection does not mean flawlessness. It means maturity, completeness, and full alignment with God's design. God works in His people to bring them to maturity so they are no longer divided, unstable, or spiritually immature. Scripture calls believers to grow into fullness, reflecting Christ in character and conduct (Matthew 5:48 AMP; Ephesians 4:13 AMP).

Maturity stabilizes identity and authority.

5. Formation Into the Image and Likeness of God

God's ultimate purpose is restoration of His image and likeness in humanity. Through obedience, holiness, and maturity, believers are transformed inwardly and outwardly. Scripture declares that believers are being transformed into the same image from glory to glory by the Spirit of the Lord (Genesis 1:26 AMP; 2 Corinthians 3:18 AMP).

The Goshen Factor protects this formation process.

6. Walking as a Mature Soldier-Servant of the Lord of Hosts

Under Jehovah Sabaoth, believers are not merely protected. They are trained, matured, and commissioned. A mature soldier-servant reflects God's character, submits to His authority, and carries His presence into the world. God equips His people to stand firm, not as spiritual infants, but as mature representatives of His Kingdom (Exodus 15:3 AMP; Ephesians 6:10–11 AMP).

Authority flows through maturity and submission.

7. Living as a Visible Witness of God's Image

A life formed in holiness and maturity becomes visible evidence of God's Kingdom. Goshen was a testimony to Egypt. Likewise, believers today reflect

God's image and authority through their conduct, peace, and obedience. God's glory is revealed through a people who live aligned with His design (Matthew 5:14–16 AMP; Romans 8:29 AMP).

Where God's image is restored, His glory is revealed.

Why This Step Completes the Goshen Walk

Protection creates space.
Provision sustains growth.
Peace guards the heart.
Holiness preserves alignment.
Maturity perfects the believer.
God's image is restored.

This is the fullness of the Goshen Factor. God protects His people so they may become like Him.

A Daily Goshen Prayer and Declaration of Alignment

A Prayer of Daily Alignment

Heavenly Father,
I thank You that You are the Lord who makes a distinction between those who belong to You and those who do not. I acknowledge that my life belongs to You through Jesus Christ. I surrender my heart, mind, and will to Your authority. I choose to live aligned with Your covenant and under Your governance (Exodus 11:7 AMP).

I thank You for the blood of Jesus that speaks on my behalf, establishes covenant, restrains accusation, and secures my redemption. I trust in the finished work of Christ and receive forgiveness, protection, and peace through His sacrifice (Hebrews 12:24 AMP; Colossians 1:20 AMP).

Holy Spirit, lead me into truth, empower my obedience, and form Christ within me. Shape my character, mature my faith, and transform me into the image and likeness of God. Keep my heart sensitive and my life holy before You (John 16:13 AMP; 2 Corinthians 3:18 AMP).

I trust You for provision, peace, and purpose. I reject fear, compromise, and self-reliance. I choose obedience, holiness, and maturity as I walk under Your authority. Guard me by Your presence and establish Your will in my life (Philippians 4:6–7 AMP; Leviticus 20:26 AMP).

I declare that my life is governed by You. Where You rule, peace remains, protection stands, and purpose is fulfilled. I thank You for establishing Goshen in my life today.
Amen.

The Goshen Declaration

A Confession of Covenant Position

I declare that I belong to God.
I am redeemed by the blood of Jesus.
I am marked by covenant and covered by divine authority.

I declare that God has drawn a line around my life.
Judgment is restrained.
Darkness is silenced.
Fear has no voice against me.

I am no longer a slave.
I am a redeemed soldier-servant of the Most High God.
I live under the authority of Jehovah Sabaoth.

I walk in obedience, holiness, and maturity.
I am being transformed into the image and

likeness of God.
I am seated with Christ in heavenly places, above fear, accusation, and defeat (Ephesians 2:6 AMP).

Provision sustains me.
Peace guards me.
Purpose directs me.

This is my covenant position.
This is my declaration.
This is the Goshen Factor at work in my life.

CLOSING NOTE FOR THE BOOKLET

Goshen is not a place you visit.
It is a position you live in.

Where God governs, Goshen exists.

An Invitation Into Covenant

God still draws lines of distinction. He still marks ownership. He still restrains destruction. Through Jesus Christ, you can step into covenant, protection, and purpose.

A Prayer of Salvation

Heavenly Father,
I acknowledge that I am a sinner in need of Your grace.
I believe that Jesus Christ is the Son of God, that He died for my sins, and that He rose again.
I receive His blood as my covering and His sacrifice as my redemption.
Forgive me, cleanse me, and make me new.
I surrender my life to You and confess Jesus Christ as Lord.
Lead me into Your purpose and keep me under Your authority.
Amen.

www.ingramcontent.com/pod-product-compliance
Lightning Source LLC
LaVergne TN
LVHW090618110826
845146LV00001B/445

* 9 7 9 8 9 9 4 0 1 6 0 7 7 *